THE Life of JESUS
PARTICIPANT'S GUIDE

The Deeper Connections Series

The Miracles of Jesus

The Last Days of Jesus

The Forgiveness of Jesus

The Life of Jesus

Deeper CONNECTIONS

The Life of JESUS

PARTICIPANT'S GUIDE

Six In-depth Studies Connecting the Bible to Life

Matt Williams
General Editor

Deeper Connections:
The Life of Jesus Participant's Guide
© 2009, 2018 Matt Williams
Rose Publishing, LLC
P. O. Box 3473
Peabody, Massachusetts 01961-3473 USA
www.hendricksonrose.com

Download a free Leader's Guide at www.hendricksonrose.com/lifeofjesus-guides

Cover design: Tammy Johnson
Interior Design: Mark Sheeres

Printed in the United States of America

Contents

Preface

We all know Christians who are bored with Bible study—not because the Bible is boring, but because they haven't been introduced to its meaning in its first-century context and how that is significant for our lives today. When we begin to understand some of these "deeper connections"—both to the first century and to the twenty-first century—our lives are transformed.

The idea for the Deeper Connections series grew out of a concern that far too many Bible studies lack depth and solid biblical application. We wanted a Bible study series that was written and taught by Biblical experts who could also communicate that material in a *clear, practical, understandable* manner. The Deeper Connections teachers have one foot in the historical, biblical text and the other in the modern world; they not only have written numerous books, they have many years of pastoral experience. When they teach in the local church, they often hear comments such as, "Wow, I've never heard it explained that way before." Unfortunately, that's because, until recently, Bible professors usually spent most of their time writing books for other professors, or occasionally for pastors, and the layperson in the church had little access to this biblical knowledge. Deeper Connections seeks to remedy this by bringing the best in biblical scholarship directly to small groups and Sunday school classes through the popular medium of DVD.

Don't be scared by the word "deeper"—deeper does not mean that these studies are hard to understand. It simply means that we are attempting to get at the true meaning of the biblical text, which involves investigating the historical, religious, and social background of first-century Jewish culture and their Greek and Roman neighbors. If we fail to study and understand this background, then we also fail to understand the deeper and true meaning of the Bible.

After making deeper connections to the biblical texts, the teachers then apply that text to life in the twenty-first century. This is where a deeper look into the text really pays off. Life-application in the church today has sometimes been a bit shallow and many times unrelated to the biblical passage itself. In this series, the practical application derives directly out of the biblical text.

So, to borrow the alternate title of *The Hobbit*, J. R. R. Tolkien's bestselling classic, we invite you to join us on an adventure to "there and back again"! Your life won't be the same as a result.

About the Video Teachers

Dr. Darrell Bock is research professor of New Testament Studies at Dallas Theological Seminary in Dallas, Texas. An editor-at-large for *Christianity Today*, he speaks and teaches on the person of Jesus both nationally and internationally. Darrell is the author of more than twenty books, including a *New York Times* nonfiction bestseller and two commentaries on the gospel of Luke.

Dr. Gary Burge is professor of New Testament at Wheaton College in Wheaton, Illinois, and a sought-after conference speaker. His experiences in Beirut, Lebanon, in the early 1970s when civil war broke out have helped him to see how valuable it is to understand the world of the Middle East in order to correctly understand the biblical world of Jesus. Gary is the author of many books, including a commentary on the gospel of John.

Dr. Scott Duvall is professor of New Testament at Ouachita Baptist University in Little Rock, Arkansas, where he has won the Outstanding Faculty Award four times. He has pastored various churches, and presently is co-pastor of Fellowship Church in Arkadelphia, Arkansas. Scott has written many books on how to interpret, preach, and apply the Bible.

Prof. Susan Hecht is instructor of New Testament at Denver Seminary in Denver, Colorado. She is currently completing a doctorate in New Testament from Trinity Evangelical Divinity School, before which she ministered on college campuses with Campus Crusade for Christ for twenty years in Colorado, Oregon, and North Carolina. Susan has written on the topic of ministry to postmoderns.

Dr. Mark Strauss is professor of New Testament at Bethel Seminary in San Diego, California. He is a frequent preacher at San Diego area churches and has served in three interim pastorates. Mark is the author of many books, including a commentary on the gospel of Luke and *Four Portraits, One Jesus: An Introduction to Jesus and the Gospels.*

Dr. Matt Williams is associate professor of New Testament at Talbot School of Theology, Biola University, La Mirada, California. A former missionary to Spain, Matt preaches and teaches in churches throughout the United States and Spain. He is general editor of *Biblioteca Teológica Vida*, *Colección Teológica Contemporánea*, and *What the New Testament Authors Really Cared About*, and is the author of two books on the Gospels.

Host **Margaret Feinberg** (www.margaretfeinberg.com) is a popular speaker at churches and leading conferences such as Fusion, Catalyst, and National Pastors Convention. Named one of the "Thirty Emerging Voices" of Christian leaders under age forty by *Charisma* magazine, she has written more than 700 articles and a dozen books, including *The Organic God* and *The Sacred Echo.* She lives in Colorado.

SESSION 1

Birthday Surprises

Birth of Jesus
(Luke 2:1 – 16)

Dr. Mark Strauss

Today in the town of David a Savior has been born to you; he is Christ the Lord. This will be a sign to you: You will find a baby wrapped in cloths and lying in a manger.

Luke 2:11 – 12

The history of God's people has now reached its long-awaited goal.

Donald Hagner

INTRODUCTION

Video Opener from Israel

Scripture Reading: Luke 2:1–16, followed by a prayer that God will open your heart as you study his Word

Location of Passage: Bethlehem

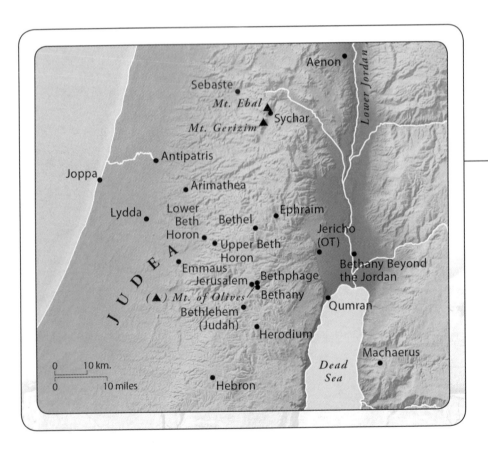

MAKING DEEPER CONNECTIONS TO THE BIBLE

I can't think of two better words to describe the first Christmas two thousand years ago than these two words: "traditions" and "surprises."

Video Teaching #1 Notes

NOTE: In each session of this participant's guide, the "Video Teaching Notes" sections give an outline of the video teaching, with additional quotes and biblical passages. Educators have proved that the teacher's main points will be remembered better if you follow along in the guide and see the main teaching points, and even better if you jot down notes in the spaces provided.

Location of Video Teaching: Near a cave

Christmas traditions

> ### DID YOU KNOW?
>
> The tradition that Jesus was born in a cave dates from as early as AD 135.
>
> Peter Walker

Christmas surprises

Traditional location of Jesus' birth, Church of the Nativity

Israel's traditions

Michelangelo's David

Promise of a Messiah from
David's line

> The LORD declares to you [David] that the LORD himself will establish a house for you: When your days are over and you rest with your fathers, I will raise up your offspring to succeed you, who will come from your own body, and I will establish his kingdom. He is the one who will build a house for my Name, and I will establish the throne of his kingdom forever.
>
> 2 Samuel 7:11 – 13
>
>
>
> He will be great and will be called the Son of the Most High. The Lord God will give him the throne of his father David, and he will reign over the house of Jacob forever; his kingdom will never end.
>
> Luke 1:32–35

Promise of a Messiah who would reign in justice and righteousness

The Spirit of the Lord will rest on him — the Spirit of wisdom and of understanding, the Spirit of counsel and of power.... With righteousness he will judge the needy, with justice he will give decisions for the poor of the earth.

Isaiah 11:2, 4

My soul glorifies the Lord and my spirit rejoices in God my Savior ... he has scattered those who are proud in their inmost thoughts. He has brought down rulers from their thrones but has lifted up the humble. He has filled the hungry with good things but has sent the rich away empty.

Luke 1:46–47, 51–53

Promise of a Messiah who would save his people

[The Lord] has raised up a horn of salvation for us in the house of his servant David (as he said through his holy prophets of long ago), salvation from our enemies and from the hand of all who hate us — to show mercy to our fathers and to remember his holy covenant.

Luke 1:69–72

Israel's surprises

A king born in a stable (humility)

DID YOU KNOW?

Mary is in her early teens, as this is when Jewish girls usually would marry.

Darrell Bock

Mary and Joseph

In Old Testament times, the penalty for adultery was stoning. But by the first century (when Roman rule had abolished Jewish death penalties) divorce was the normal course.

R. T. France

Bethlehem

In those days Caesar Augustus issued a decree that a census should be taken of the entire Roman world. So Joseph also went up from the town of Nazareth in Galilee to Judea, to Bethlehem the town of David, because he belonged to the house and line of David. He went there to register with Mary, who was pledged to be married to him and was expecting a child. While they were there, the time came for the baby to be born, and she gave birth to her firstborn, a son. She wrapped him in cloths and placed him in a *manger*, because there was no room for them in the inn.

Luke 2:1, 4–7

A Messiah rejected
by the powerful, but
worshiped by the lowly

Shepherds and the magi

And there were shepherds living out in the fields nearby, keeping watch over their flocks at night. An angel of the Lord appeared to them, and the glory of the Lord shone around them, and they were terrified. But the angel said to them, "Do not be afraid. I bring you good news of great joy that will be for all the people. Today in the town of David a Savior has been born to you; he is Christ the Lord. This will be a sign to you: You will find a baby wrapped in cloths and lying in a manger."

Luke 2:8–12

The shepherds were welcome at the manger. The outcasts became honored guests.

Kenneth Bailey

> After Jesus was born in Bethlehem in Judea, during the time of King Herod, Magi from the east came to Jerusalem and asked, "Where is the one who has been born king of the Jews? We saw his star in the east and have come to worship him."
>
>
> Matthew 2:1–2

Herod the Great

> When Herod realized that he had been outwitted by the Magi, he was furious, and he gave orders to kill all the boys in Bethlehem and its vicinity who were two years old and under, in accordance with the time he had learned from the Magi.
>
>
> Matthew 2:16

> As Herod grew older, he became increasingly paranoid. He had numerous sons, wives, and others put to death because he feared plots to overthrow him.
>
> Craig Blomberg

A Messiah who would suffer and die before he would reign

> For even the Son of Man did not come to be served, but to serve, and to give his life as a ransom for many.
>
> Mark 10:45

VIDEO DISCUSSION #1: MAKING DEEPER CONNECTIONS TO THE BIBLE

NOTE: In each session of the participant's guide, "Video Discussion #1" mainly focuses on understanding the *meaning of the biblical text* in all its depth and fullness. Please see the leader's guide for the amount of time your group should discuss the following questions before moving on to Video Teaching #2, Connecting the Bible to Life.

1. Looking back at the Bible passage and your video teaching notes, what did you learn that you did not know previously? Consider specifically:

   - The promise of a messiah from the line of David

   - The promise of a messiah who would reign in righteousness

   - The surprise of being born in a "stable" (what kind of a "stable" do you think Jesus was born in?)

2. When you celebrate Christmas each year, do you think about the *surprising* nature of the way that God fulfilled his Old Testament *promises* to Israel, or do you think more about presents, blessings, parties with family and friends, etc.? How does it help you to know the Old Testament background of Jesus' coming as the messianic King?

3. Imagine that you were Mary or Joseph. Do you think that you would have done the same things that they did—Mary agreeing to mother the son of God, and Joseph to stay with Mary and adopt Jesus as his own son? What kind of shame would you have faced in your community? Would it have been worth it?

4. What do you think God was trying to say by using the lowly, the rejected, the outcasts to play important roles at the birth of Jesus? Can we draw any conclusions from this as to whom God might use today? Do you understand that God can use anyone, no matter what their position in life?

CONNECTING THE BIBLE TO LIFE

What will our response be when we are surprised by the presence of Jesus?

Video Teaching #2 Notes

Traditions and surprises

God's promises never fail

Promise to meet our needs

And my God will meet all your needs according to his glorious riches in Christ Jesus.

Philippians 4:19

Promise of peace and contentment through difficult times

> Do not be anxious about anything, but in everything, by prayer and petition, with thanksgiving, present your requests to God. And the peace of God, which transcends all understanding, will guard your hearts and your minds in Christ Jesus.
>
> Philippians 4:6–7

Promise of salvation

God cares for the humble, the lowly

> The realization of eschatological salvation means blessing for all the nations and not simply Israel — in accord with God's promise to Abraham.
>
> Donald Hagner

Jesus' ministry to the lowly

There are no more "normal Joes" in ancient culture than shepherds.

Darrell Bock

God wants us to approach him with a humble heart

God wants us to reach out to the needs of others

Physical and spiritual renewal go hand-in-hand

> But seek first his kingdom and his righteousness, and all these things will be given to you as well.
>
> Matthew 6:33

The surprise of Jesus

VIDEO DISCUSSION #2: CONNECTING THE BIBLE TO LIFE

NOTE: While "Video Discussion #1" mainly focused on the meaning of the biblical text, "Video Discussion #2" in each session mainly focuses on *applying* the biblical text to our lives today. Please see the leader's guide for the amount of time your group should discuss the following questions.

1. Jesus' birth narrative illustrates that God faithfully fulfilled his Old Testament promises. How have you found God's promise-keeping to be true in your own life? How have you seen him meet your needs? How have you experienced his peace? Do you think that, just like in the birth of Jesus, God fulfills his promises in *surprising* ways? Explain your answer.

2. God cares for the lowly and the poor. We see this over and over again in Jesus' birth, as the lowly understand its significance, while the powerful do not. What does it look like to approach God with a heart of humble dependence as opposed to approaching him with pride? How are you personally doing at this?

3. Why do you think that those who understood the significance of Jesus' birth went to worship him? How can we worship him today, since we can't take him a gift like the magi did?

4. In the birth narratives, God pursued and told the good news to Mary, Joseph, the magi, the shepherds, and even Simeon and Anna. God still pursues people today. Consider for a few moments as a group what your lives would be like today if God were not a God who pursues and loves you.

MAKING DEEPER CONNECTIONS IN YOUR OWN LIFE

Personal reflection studies to do on your own

Day One

1. Read Matthew 1:18–2:12.

2. Worship is a frequent theme in the gospel accounts of Jesus' birth. When you think of Christmas, do you think about worship as one of its most important themes?

3. Think about the cost paid by the various people who participated in the events surrounding Jesus' birth: Jesus left his heavenly home to become human; Mary and Joseph suffered shame for having a child before marriage; the shepherds had to leave their flocks; the magi traveled an estimated nine hundred miles in search of a new king. What does it cost you to worship Jesus? Are you willing to pay the price?

Day Two

1. Read Luke 1:26–38.

2. Joy is a continual theme surrounding the birth of Jesus (see Luke 1:14, 44, 58; 2:10). Is joy a characteristic of your life? If not, what/who is robbing you of your joy? Spend some time in prayer asking God to fill your life with more joy.

3. People make New Year's resolutions all the time, but how often does someone resolve to pursue God and know him more fully? Those who understand both the traditions and surprises of Jesus' birth will want to pursue with their whole life this child who grew up to be the Savior of the world! Is this your resolution? If so, what would that look like on a day-by-day basis?

Day Three

1. Read Luke 1:46–56.

2. The incarnation—the birth of Jesus—means that God is with us. Because God became like us, it means that he understands us. Jesus has been tempted as we are, though without sin (Hebrews 4:15). He can sympathize with our difficulties and he is right now praying for us. Spend some time giving your temptations and troubles to the Lord, and ask him to empower you.

3. The ultimate reason that Jesus came to earth was to redeem us. Redemption, however, is costly. Even before the manger, the cross is in view. Skim through the birth narratives and find as many allusions to suffering as you can (for example, Herod killing all boys under age two). It was Jesus' suffering and death that brought us redemption: by his wounds we are healed! Thank him, even now as we study the birth of Jesus, that he came and was willing to pay the price for you.

Day Four

1. Read Luke 2:21–39.

2. One of the most impactful Christmas sermons I have ever heard was called, "Let the Baby Grow Up." You see, if we keep Jesus as this small, innocent, eight-pound baby, he makes no demands on our lives. Have you allowed the baby to grow up? What demands does the grown-up Jesus make on your life?

3. Skim through the birth narratives of Matthew and Luke and list all of the titles given to Jesus while yet a baby: Messiah, King, Lord, etc. Then meditate on each title and the demands upon your life that each one makes. For example, the fact that Jesus is King means that we are his subordinates, his servants, owing him our full allegiance.

Day Five

1. Read Luke 2:1–16 one more time.

2. Pray through the entire passage verse by verse, allowing the deeper meaning that you have discovered to lead you as you pray. Ask the Spirit to continue to remind you of what you have learned and to help you apply these truths to your life. Jot down any further applications that come to mind as you pray.

3. Turn back to the discussion questions from the video teaching (Video Discussion #1, #2). If there are questions that your group did not have time to discuss or questions that you might like to think more about, use this time to review and reflect further.

John Prepares the Way

Baptism of Jesus
(Matthew 3:11 – 17)

Dr. Scott Duvall

As soon as Jesus was baptized
... a voice from heaven said,
"This is my Son, whom I love;
with him I am well pleased."

Matthew 3:16 – 17

The descent of the Spirit on Jesus
signifies his "anointing" as Messiah and his empowerment to
accomplish the task God has set
out for him.

Mark Strauss

INTRODUCTION

Video Opener from Israel

Scripture Reading: Matthew 3:11–17, followed by a prayer that God will open your heart as you study his Word

Location of Passage: Jordan River

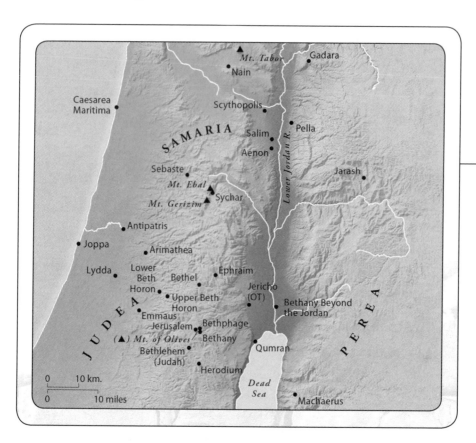

MAKING DEEPER CONNECTIONS TO THE BIBLE

After centuries of silence, God sends a prophet to anoint the Messianic King for his role as the Suffering Servant.

Video Teaching #1 Notes

Location of Video Teaching: Petit Jean State Park, Arkansas River, Little Rock, Arkansas

The Jordan River

God is sometimes silent

God breaks his silence

DID YOU KNOW?

The River Jordan is tiny; rarely is it more than fifteen yards wide.

Peter Walker

In the *fifteenth year of the reign* of Tiberius Caesar ... the *word of God* came to John *son of Zechariah* in the desert.

Luke 3:1–2

John the Baptizer

John the Baptist: John's clothes were made of camel's hair, and he had a leather belt around his waist.

Matthew 3:4

Elijah: They replied, "He was a man with a garment of hair and with a leather belt around his waist." The king said, "That was Elijah the Tishbite."

2 Kings 1:8

Judean desert

God uses the desert

> Therefore I am now going to allure her; I will lead her into the desert and speak tenderly to her. There I will give her back her vineyards, and will make the Valley of Achor a door of hope. There she will sing as in the days of her youth, as in the day she came up out of Egypt.
>
> Hosea 2:14–15

John will prepare the way for the Messiah

> A voice of one calling in the desert, "Prepare the way for the Lord, make straight paths for him."
>
> Matthew 3:3 (see Isaiah 40:3)

John baptized with water

> I will sprinkle clean water on you, and you will be clean; I will cleanse you from all your impurities and from all your idols.
>
> Ezekiel 36:25

"A baptism of repentance for the forgiveness of sins" (Mark 1:4)

And do not think you can say to yourselves, "We have Abraham as our father." I tell you that out of these stones God can raise up children for Abraham.

Matthew 3:9

"After me will come one who is more powerful than I" (Matthew 3:11)

John was giving a startling challenge to Israel — it was as though their old membership subscription had expired and everyone had to subscribe afresh.

Peter Walker

Jesus will baptize with the Holy Spirit and with fire

And afterward, I will pour out my Spirit on all people. Your sons and daughters will prophesy, your old men will dream dreams, your young men will see visions. Even on my servants, both men and women, I will pour out my Spirit in those days.

Joel 2:28–29 (see Acts 2:17–18)

Judgment

His winnowing fork is in his hand, and he will clear his threshing floor, gathering his wheat into the barn and burning up the chaff with unquenchable fire.

Matthew 3:12

Those who reject the kingdom message are already being marked out for judgment, even though the full force of that awful judgment has not yet been felt.

David Turner

Different responses to John

Confessing their sins, they were baptized by him in the Jordan River. But when he saw many of the Pharisees and Sadducees coming to where he was baptizing, he said to them: "You brood of vipers! Who warned you to flee from the coming wrath? Produce fruit in keeping with repentance."

Matthew 3:6–8

"What should we do?"

Jesus comes to the Jordan River to be baptized, John protests

The Jordan is a place of new beginnings, both for individuals and for Israel.

Peter Walker

"To fulfill all righteousness" (Matthew 3:15)

DID YOU KNOW?

The descent of the Spirit recalls well-known messianic prophecies in Isaiah which say that God will place his Spirit upon his chosen servant.

R. T. France

The heavens open, the Spirit descends

The Father speaks

> Judaism had the belief that God would occasionally speak from heaven in order to confirm some important statement.
>
> Craig Evans

"You are my Son" (Psalm 2:7)

"whom I love" (Matthew 3:17; see also Genesis 22:2)

> Then God said, "Take your son, your only son, Isaac, *whom you love*, and go to the region of Moriah. Sacrifice him there as a burnt offering on one of the mountains I will tell you about."
>
> Genesis 22:2

"with you I am well pleased"

Here is my servant, whom I uphold, my chosen one in whom I delight; I will put my Spirit on him and he will bring justice to the nations.

Isaiah 42:1

A sovereign King and a Suffering Servant

VIDEO DISCUSSION #1: MAKING DEEPER CONNECTIONS TO THE BIBLE

1. Looking back at the Bible passage and your video teaching notes, what did you learn that you did not know previously? Consider specifically:

   • The silence of God between the Old and New Testaments

- God's use of the desert

- The Old Testament expectations of water cleansing

- What John called the people to do and the importance of fruit (Luke 3:10–14)

2. What do you think John must have been thinking and feeling when Jesus came to him for baptism? Would you have been willing to baptize Jesus? Why or why not? What do you think Jesus meant when he said that John should baptize him to "fulfill all righteousness"?

3. What do you think the meaning is of each of the three phrases that the Father spoke from heaven to Jesus at his baptism? Do you think that Jesus would have known the Old Testament background and understood each phrase?

4. Do you think that the Jewish people would have easily accepted the idea of Jesus the Messiah being both a King and a Suffering Servant? Why or why not?

CONNECTING THE BIBLE TO LIFE

John the Baptist humbled himself for a "fading ministry" because he listened to the voice of God.

Video Teaching #2 Notes

John the Baptizer had a difficult life

> The way that Jesus prepares for us is not the one we want to travel. It is arduous and paved with suffering.
>
> David Garland

The American dream

Serving others: the Tour de France

A fading ministry

Sin and repentance

> Shall we go on sinning so that grace may increase? By no means! We died to sin; how can we live in it any longer? Or don't you know that all of us who were baptized into Christ Jesus were baptized into his death? We were therefore buried with him through baptism into death in order that, just as Christ was raised from the dead through the glory of the Father, we too may live a new life.
>
> Romans 6:1–4

My brother's dramatic change

> When we trust Christ we receive forgiveness from all our sin, but that does not mean we are given license to do whatever we wish.
>
> Darrell Bock

The Holy Spirit: power to overcome sin

> Now to him who is able to do immeasurably more than all we ask or imagine, according to his power that is at work within us.
>
> Ephesians 3:20

> Jesus' strength comes from his humble dependence on the same Spirit that you and I depend on.
>
> Michael Wilkins

God acted in unexpected ways in John and Jesus

God acts today in unexpected ways

God's plan is best

> We don't like to give up our appearance of importance. But knowing God's purposes for our lives and not allowing our self-promotion to get in the way will enable us to accomplish God's calling for our lives.
>
> Michael Wilkins

God is no longer silent

VIDEO DISCUSSION #2: CONNECTING THE BIBLE TO LIFE

1. Scott Duvall mentioned John the Baptist's difficult life, and we all know how Jesus' life ended. What are your honest expectations about how your life should turn out as you follow God? How much has the American dream influenced your expectations? If time permits, briefly pray that you will be influenced more by God's desires and less by your culture.

2. John called the Jewish people to repent of their sins and to bring "fruit." Can you think of any specific sins that we tend to overlook today in our churches that we might need to repent of? What specific fruit do you think the church today is good at producing? What fruit do we need to work on?

3. Matthew 3:17 says, "This is my Son, whom I love; with him I am well pleased." Why do you think that God was pleased with Jesus? What did the Father see in Jesus that made him happy? What aspects of *your* life do you think the Father is pleased with?

4. If Jesus needed the Spirit's empowerment to fulfill his ministry, how much more do we need the Spirit? Note what the Spirit does first: he drives Jesus into the desert to be tempted. The Spirit-led life is not all about us and our blessings, but about God's greater plan. Do you think that you under- or overemphasize the role of the Spirit in your own life? What specific steps do you take to ensure that you are being led by the Spirit on a daily basis?

MAKING DEEPER CONNECTIONS IN YOUR OWN LIFE

Personal reflection studies to do on your own

Day One

1. Read Matthew 3:1–17.

2. Both John and Jesus demonstrate a strong ability to become weak and lowly as they fulfill their role in God's plan. What seems to be the key to their humility, and how can we allow God to reproduce that same virtue in our lives?

3. John had a "fading ministry"—he pointed the way to Jesus by serving faithfully, even at a high cost to himself. Do you have a ministry that serves others? If not, what ministry could you do?

Day Two

1. Read Mark 1:2–11. What differences do you see in Mark's account of John and the baptism of Jesus when compared to Matthew's?

2. God was silent for centuries between the Old and New Testaments. Do you think that he is silent today? How do you hear his voice in your life? Spend some time in prayer, listening to the voice of God.

3. In this passage the Father announces from heaven that Jesus is his beloved Son. What affirming words! Do you know that you too are a beloved child of the Father? John 1:12 says, "Yet to all who received him, to those who believed in his name, he gave the right to become children of God." What does it feel like to know you're God's child? How do you experience that love? Praise God for adopting you!

Day Three

1. Read Luke 3:1–22. What differences do you see in Luke's account of John and the baptism of Jesus when compared to Matthew's and Mark's?

2. John the Baptist's message included hope and judgment, grace and truth, love and holiness. These contrasting qualities clearly reflect God's character. Both are important and neither should ever be completely divorced from the other. Which characteristic in each of these pairs of divine characteristics do you emphasize more in your life? What is the result of emphasizing hope, grace, and love at the expense of the other qualities, and vice versa?

3. Imagine that you had been one of those baptized by John in anticipation of the coming Messiah. Years later, how would you describe the whole experience to your children or grandchildren? What would you emphasize?

Day Four

1. Read John 1:26–34 and 3:22–30. What differences do you see in John's account of John (the Baptist) and the baptism of Jesus when compared to the other three Gospels?

2. The baptism marks the first stage of Jesus becoming the Suffering Servant who takes on the sins of the world. Jesus was sinless! There was no need for him to repent, but he was baptized by John in order to identify with the sinfulness of humanity. Thank Jesus for taking on *your* sins, for suffering for *you*.

3. John called the people of God to repentance of sin. What specific habits or disciplines has God used in your life to help you grow away from patterns of sin? Are there other things that you should be doing that might help you to overcome sin?

Day Five

1. Read Matthew 3:11–17 one more time.

2. Pray through the entire passage verse by verse, allowing the deeper meaning that you have discovered to lead you as you pray. Ask the Spirit to continue to remind you of what you have learned and to help you apply these truths to your life. Jot down any further applications that come to mind as you pray.

3. Turn back to the discussion questions from the video teaching (Video Discussion #1, #2). If there are questions that your group did not have time to discuss or questions that you might like to think more about, use this time to review and reflect further.

The Victorious Son of God

Temptation of Jesus (Matthew 4:1–11)

Dr. Gary Burge

Then the devil left him, and angels came and attended him.

◎ Matthew 4:11

In the desert, though we may outwardly be alone, we discover that perhaps we are not so alone after all.

◎ Peter Walker

INTRODUCTION

Video Opener from Israel

Scripture Reading: Matthew 4:1–11, followed by a prayer that God will open your heart as you study his Word

Location of Passage: Judean Desert

MAKING DEEPER CONNECTIONS TO THE BIBLE

Jesus was tempted by Satan himself to trade in his future kingdom for the kingdoms of this world.

Video Teaching #1 Notes

Location of Video Teaching: Downtown Chicago

Jordan River

The Jordan River

The baptism of Jesus

> The baptism of Jesus marks the call of Jesus to his public ministry, a call accompanied by the gift of the Holy Spirit and confirmed by a voice from heaven.
>
> Leon Morris

God's voice, the Spirit's anointing

> I have installed my King on Zion, my holy hill. I will proclaim the decree of the LORD: He said to me, "You are my Son; today I have become your Father."
>
> Psalm 2:6–7

Recap of Israel's history

Jesus is reliving a portion of Israel's history

Tell al-Kharrar, possible site of Jesus' baptism

Jesus as the new Israel

While God's son Israel failed when tested in the desert, Jesus, the true Son of God, succeeds.

Mark Strauss

Moses on Mount Sinai

DID YOU KNOW?

Jews commonly practiced fasting in order to spend more time in prayer and to develop greater spiritual receptivity.

Craig Blomberg

When I went up on the mountain to receive the tablets of stone, the tablets of the covenant that the LORD had made with you, I stayed on the mountain forty days and forty nights; I ate no bread and drank no water.

Deuteronomy 9:9

Deuteronomy chapters 1–10

> Remember how the LORD your God led you all the way in the desert these forty years, to humble you and to test you in order to know what was in your heart, whether or not you would keep his commands.
>
> Deuteronomy 8:2

The desert

DID YOU KNOW?

The wilderness was sometimes viewed as the domain of evil spirits.

Craig Evans

If you do well, people and angels will bless you and God will be glorified among you. The devil will flee from you; the wild animals will be afraid of you, and the angels will stand by you.

The Testament of Nephtali 8:4

Jesus meets Satan

Jesus' three temptations

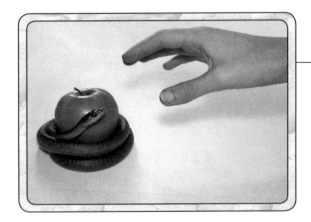

No offer is great enough to persuade Jesus to abandon his Father.

Darrell Bock

Jesus' defense: Deuteronomy

"If you are the Son of God"

Will Jesus use his powers of sonship for God and his work, or will he use these powers for his own self-interest?

Gary Burge

First temptation: bread from stone

He humbled you, causing you to hunger and then feeding you with manna, which neither you nor your fathers had known, to teach you that man does not live on bread alone but on every word that comes from the mouth of the LORD.

Deuteronomy 8:3

Second temptation: jump from the temple

Do not test the LORD your God as you did at Massah.

Deuteronomy 6:16

Third temptation: the kingdoms of the world

Jesus will take only the road God asks him to follow. He will not take any shortcuts.

Darrell Bock

Fear the LORD your God, serve him only and take your oaths in his name. Do not follow other gods, the gods of the peoples around you.

Deuteronomy 6:13–14

Jesus will be victorious, but not for self-interests

The devil offered Jesus a shortcut — to bypass the suffering of the cross. But before he sits on his royal throne, he must hang on the cross.

Michael Wilkins

The temptations
continued: the cross

> He forgave us all our sins ... he took it away, nailing it to the cross. And
> having disarmed the powers and authorities, he made a public spectacle of
> them, triumphing over them by the cross.
>
> Colossians 2:13 – 15

VIDEO DISCUSSION #1: MAKING DEEPER CONNECTIONS TO THE BIBLE

1. Looking back at the Bible passage and your video teaching
   notes, what did you learn that you did not know previously?
   Consider specifically:

   • Jesus reliving Israel's history

   • Jesus' use of Deuteronomy in the temptations

- The meaning of each of the three temptations

- The significance of the desert in the first century

2. Each time that Satan tempted Jesus, Jesus used Scripture to rebuke him. Do you think that Christians today know the Bible well enough to be able to use it to combat temptations? Consider your own temptations: When do you seem most vulnerable to them? What strategies have you used to overcome them? If you have used Scripture successfully, what specific texts have been helpful to you?

3. Satan tempted Jesus to abandon the Father in order to gain personal wealth and power. What offers does Satan make today that might cause Christians you know to consider abandoning God? What offers tempt you?

4. The devil's temptation to turn stones into bread was not inherently evil. But Jesus knew that it was God's will for him to be hungry at that time. How did he know this? Do you think the forty days of fasting played a role in Jesus knowing the Father's will? How do you find God's will for your life? How do you tell the difference between Satan's temptations and God's blessings?

CONNECTING THE BIBLE TO LIFE

God places his people in the desert, then stands by us — honing our faith through every one of our experiences there.

Video Teaching #2 Notes

Judean desert

God's voice is clearer in the desert

Remember how the LORD your God led you all the way in the desert these forty years, to humble you and to test you in order to know what was in your heart, whether or not you would keep his commands.

Deuteronomy 8:2

Old Testament heroes
in the desert

No godly man or woman can avoid the desert

If I am to grow spiritually, I can expect trials.

Darrell Bock

The meaning of Jesus' temptations

Fundamental temptation: power

> Beware lest you say in your heart, "My power and the might of my hand have gotten me this wealth." You shall remember the LORD your God for he is the one who gives you power to get wealth.
>
> Deuteronomy 8:17–18 ESV

The temptation was ultimately about seizing power on one's own apart from God's promise and provision.

Darrell Bock

Those who have much are tempted

Satan regularly tempts Christians with the success syndrome, empire building, or alleged guarantees of health and wealth. But the devil's price is damning.

Craig Blomberg

Identify and defeat Satan's temptations

Resist the devil

Resist the devil, and he will flee from you.

James 4:7

Be self-controlled and alert. Your enemy the devil prowls around like a roaring lion looking for someone to devour. Resist him, standing firm in the faith.

1 Peter 5:8–9

Using Scripture to defeat temptation

Temptations involve the twisting of reality, so the antidote comes from the *truth* of Scripture.

Michael Wilkins

Using the Spirit to defeat temptation

> So I say, live by the Spirit, and you will not gratify the desires of the sinful nature.
>
> Galatians 5:16

Satan's temptations continue today

Will we be seduced?

As powerful as Satan may be, and as frail as Jesus must be because of the extended fasting and the intensity of the temptations, Jesus vanquishes him with a word.

Michael Wilkins

VIDEO DISCUSSION #2: CONNECTING THE BIBLE TO LIFE

1. Gary Burge said that all of us go through the desert to learn from God. Have you been in the desert? What did you learn there? Do you think that you could have learned that same lesson without having gone through the desert?

2. Gary Burge mentioned that the central theme of Satan's temptations was power. Do you think that most Christians today are tempted by power? Do you think that most Christians recognize temptations for power? Can you give some examples? Is this your hardest temptation? Why or why not?

3. Jesus resisted Satan's temptations by relying on Scripture. Is that your normal way of fighting off temptations? Does such a response to temptation require Christians to learn Scripture and memorize it, such as Jesus did? Do you think most Christians today memorize Scripture enough to make it a powerful weapon? What about you?

4. Jesus also resisted Satan's temptations through the power of the Holy Spirit (recall that the Spirit led Jesus into the desert, see Matthew 4:1). Is relying on the Spirit's power your normal way of fighting off temptations? What does that look like for you? Do you think it is difficult to determine if it is the Spirit leading you versus the enemy? How do you tell the difference?

MAKING DEEPER CONNECTIONS IN YOUR OWN LIFE

Personal reflection studies to do on your own

Day One

1. Read Hebrews 4:14–5:2.

2. This passage tells us that Jesus is the great high priest who "sympathizes with our weaknesses," is "without sin," gives "mercy" and "grace," and "deals gently" with us. Thank Jesus in prayer for his ministry on our behalf, then note below specific instances when you have experienced any of these benefits in your own life.

3. Because Jesus is the understanding high priest, this passage also instructs us to "hold firmly to the faith" and to "approach the throne of grace with confidence." When you think about Jesus' grace toward you, does it motivate you to "hold firmly to the faith"? Or does it allow you to be a little more casual in your own sin?

Day Two

1. Read John 10:1–5.

2. We often think that God's voice must sound like thunder—loud and deep. Yet when God spoke to Samuel, Samuel thought that Eli was speaking to him. (So, on at least that occasion, God's voice sounded a lot like Eli's.) Have you ever wondered what God's voice sounds like when he speaks to you? Is it a voice that is different than your own, or could it be a thought that you have in your mind, or does he speak to you through other people?

3. How can we hear Jesus' voice today, given all the sounds around us (TV, Ipods, cell phones, Internet, etc.)? Can you confidently claim to hear Jesus' voice? Can you distinguish it from the enemy's voice, as Jesus says that his followers will be able to do? Once you hear his voice, do you follow the Good Shepherd wherever he leads you?

Day Three

1. Read Mark 1:12–13. Compare Mark's temptation narrative to Matthew's. Why do you think that Mark did not write very much about Jesus' temptations?

2. We cannot forget the ending of this story: Satan loses. Jesus was victorious, and the message of the New Testament is that we also can have victory in Christ. First Corinthians 10:13 puts it this way: "No temptation has seized you except what is common to man. And God is faithful; he will not let you be tempted beyond what you can bear. But when you are tempted, he will also provide a way out so that you can stand up under it." Satan is certainly tempting you in some way today. Pray about your current temptations, and ask God to show you "the way of escape."

3. Often we think that Satan tempts us at our low points. But Jesus' temptation came right after his baptism, a high point. It seems reasonable to conclude that Satan takes a keen interest in those who have recently had a fresh experience with God. Have you seen this to be true in your life? Perhaps we should follow Jesus' example and spend concentrated time in prayer and fasting at the critical points of our life so that, like him, we have the strength to resist the temptation.

Day Four

1. Read Luke 4:1–13. Compare Luke's temptation narrative to Matthew's.

2. Satan basically says, "Empower yourself, take what you can, conquer others, control"—at home, at work, wherever. The test of God is whether we will see our first role in the world as service. "The Son of Man did not come to be served, but to serve" (Mark 10:45). Is abuse of power a temptation for you? If so, in what ways?

3. The temptation narrative ends by stating, "Then the devil left him, and angels came and attended him" (Matthew 4:11). What do you think the angels did when they "attended" to Jesus? Hebrews 1:14 says, "Are not all angels ministering spirits sent to serve those who will inherit salvation?" How do you think angels might serve God's people today?

Day Five

1. Read Matthew 4:1–11 one more time.

2. Pray through the entire passage verse by verse, allowing the deeper meaning that you have discovered to lead you as you pray. Ask the Spirit to continue to remind you of what you have learned and to help you apply these truths to your life. Jot down any further applications that come to mind as you pray.

3. Turn back to the discussion questions from the video teaching (Video Discussion #1, #2). If there are questions that your group did not have time to discuss or questions that you might like to think more about, use this time to review and reflect further.

Fishing with the Master

Jesus Calls Disciples
(Luke 5:1–11)

Dr. Darrell Bock

Then Jesus said to Simon, "Don't be afraid; from now on you will catch men." So they pulled their boats up on shore, left everything and followed him.

◎ Luke 5:10 – 11

Instead of sifting among "applicants" (like typical rabbis), Jesus took the initiative to command people to follow him.

◎ Craig Blomberg

INTRODUCTION

Video Opener from Israel

Scripture Reading: Luke 5:1–11, followed by a prayer that God will open your heart as you study his Word

Location of Passage: Alongside the Sea of Galilee

MAKING DEEPER CONNECTIONS TO THE BIBLE

To start a movement, we would seek the best and the brightest, but that is not what Jesus did.

Video Teaching #1 Notes

Location of Video Teaching: Dallas Theological Seminary

Jesus launched a reform movement

Sea of Galilee

Fishing

Fishing boats

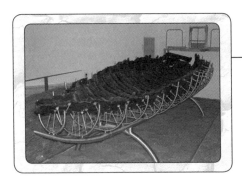

Best time to fish

When he had finished speaking, he said to Simon, "Put out into deep water, and let down the nets for a catch." Simon answered, "Master, we've worked hard all night and haven't caught anything. But because you say so, I will let down the nets."

Luke 5:4–5

Peter's response to the catch of fish

> When they had done so, they caught such a large number of fish that their nets began to break.... When Simon Peter saw this, he fell at Jesus' knees and said, "Go away from me, Lord; I am a sinful man!"
>
> Luke 5:6, 8

Only an agent of God could have produced such a catch in the middle of the day.

Darrell Bock

Jesus' response to Peter

> Then Jesus said to Simon, "Don't be afraid; from now on you will catch men."
>
> Luke 5:10

Two opposing theologies

To be a disciple means accepting Jesus' demands unconditionally.

David Garland

The deeper meaning of the miraculous

The humility of the centurion

Lord, don't trouble yourself, for I do not deserve to have you come under my roof. That is why I did not even consider myself worthy to come to you. But say the word, and my servant will be healed.

Luke 7:6–7

Sensitive to Jesus' Jewishness, power, and authority

Twelve disciples

> Jesus said to them, "I tell you the truth, at the renewal of all things, when the Son of Man sits on his glorious throne, you who have followed me will also sit on twelve thrones, judging the twelve tribes of Israel.
>
> Matthew 19:28

That they left family and occupation was a radical move, given the cultural responsibility to submit to parents and fulfill family obligations.

Craig Blomberg

Renewal of Judaism

DID YOU KNOW?

At the time of Jesus only two and a half tribes remained — the tribes of Judah, Benjamin and half the tribe of Levi. The other nine and a half tribes were lost in 722 BC when Samaria fell and were scattered in exile among the Gentiles.

Robert Stein

VIDEO DISCUSSION #1: MAKING DEEPER CONNECTIONS TO THE BIBLE

1. Do you think that most Christians today meet the number one requirement of a disciple, that of humility? What do you think a humble Christian looks like? Do you see such people in your local church?

2. Why do you think that Peter responded to the miraculous catch of fish by dropping down at the feet of Jesus and stating, "Go away from me, Lord; I am a sinful man!"?

3. If you were launching a reform movement, do you think that you would have started it with just twelve disciples? Do you think that you would have started it with people like fishermen and tax collectors? Explain.

4. What do you think of Jesus' theology of discipleship: that he can and will use anyone who is humble? Does that mean that he could use you?

CONNECTING THE BIBLE TO LIFE

A humble heart listens to God and is empowered by him in the process of fishing for people.

Video Teaching #2 Notes

Unique person

> **DID YOU KNOW?**
>
> What is striking is that Jesus calls them to "follow me." Prophets did not call people to follow themselves but to follow God!
>
> David Garland

Unique calling

And how can they believe in the one of whom they have not heard? And how can they hear without someone preaching to them?

Romans 10:14

Unique requirement

Follow my example, as I follow the example of Christ.

1 Corinthians 11:1

Humble ambassadors

We are therefore Christ's ambassadors, as though God were making his appeal through us. We implore you on Christ's behalf: Be reconciled to God.

2 Corinthians 5:20

Fishing nets in antiquity

Evangelism aided by God

A little faith in a big God can accomplish extraordinary things.

Mark Strauss

Leaving everything to be a disciple

"Come, follow me," Jesus said, "and I will make you fishers of men." At once they left their nets and followed him. When he had gone a little farther, he saw James son of Zebedee and his brother John in a boat, preparing their nets. Without delay he called them, and they left their father Zebedee in the boat with the hired men and followed him.

Mark 1:17–20

Whatever our profession, discipleship means that our priority is to join with Jesus in reaching our daily world with the good news of life in the kingdom of God.

Michael Wilkins

Calling humble learners

VIDEO DISCUSSION #2: CONNECTING THE BIBLE TO LIFE

1. What does it mean to be an ambassador to a foreign country? What qualifications does that person need; what responsibilities and authority does he or she have? Now discuss these same questions for a Christian, each of whom is an ambassador for the God of the universe?

2. If all Christians took their role as God's ambassador seriously, what do you think would happen, both to us and to those around us — our families, our churches, our communities, the world?

3. Simon and Andrew had literal nets that they had to leave in order to follow Jesus. What was the "net" that you had to drop when you came to know Jesus? Have you gone back and picked it up again?

4. What do you think it means to "leave everything" to follow Jesus? Is this hard to do? Why or why not?

MAKING DEEPER CONNECTIONS IN YOUR OWN LIFE

Personal reflection studies to do on your own

Day One

1. Read Mark 1:14–20.

2. What do you think went through the minds of Simon and Andrew as Jesus called them? Were they excited, skeptical? Did they realize that this was Jesus the Messiah fulfilling Old Testament prophecy? Do you think that they had to know everything about Jesus in order to decide to follow him?

3. Darrell Bock said that our unique calling as followers of Jesus is not just to gather together to talk about God, but to go out and reach other people with his message. Do the Christians in your church have a good balance between studying about God and going out and telling others about him?

Day Two

1. Read Matthew 4:12–25.

2. Darrell Bock said that Jesus is a "unique person," meaning he is special and above all others. In today's culture many people pride themselves for being accepting and tolerant of others, yet have become intolerant of truth, particularly the truth claims of Christianity. Can Christians who want to live out God's commands be tolerant? If so, how is tolerance defined by the church? What is "biblical" tolerance?

3. What specific characteristics of Jesus' life do you think appeared most attractive to Simon and Andrew? What attributes of his character do you find attractive and desire to imitate? Why?

Day Three

1. Read John 1:35–50.

2. Just as Jesus called Simon and Andrew, he calls us to enter into a life with a higher purpose, to be "fishers of people." Can we think of anything more important than following Jesus and winning souls? Would strangers be able to examine your life for one day and determine that you are living differently because of Jesus? What would they point to?

3. Do you believe that there are "Simons and Andrews" all around us — in our workplaces, schools, and communities? What role might you play in their coming to know Christ and his kingdom? Have you ever "called" others to follow Jesus?

Day Four

1. Read Matthew 10:1–20.

2. Spend some time today thinking about the humility that Jesus seeks in his disciples. What changes would you need to make in your life to make humility a number one priority?

3. As you become more acquainted with Jesus, do you find yourself more compelled to follow his example? Or do doubts and resistance remain? Bottom line, do you trust Jesus more now than when you first met him?

Day Five

1. Read Luke 5:1–11 one more time.

2. Pray through the entire passage verse by verse, allowing the deeper meaning that you have discovered to lead you as you pray. Ask the Spirit to continue to remind you of what you have learned and to help you apply these truths to your life. Jot down any further applications that come to mind as you pray.

3. Turn back to the discussion questions from the video teaching (Video Discussion #1, #2). If there are questions that your group did not have time to discuss or questions that you might like to think more about, use this time to review and reflect further.

Disease Conquered

Jesus Heals the Sick (Matthew 9:27–34)

Prof. Susan Hecht

As Jesus went on from there, two blind men followed him, calling out, "Have mercy on us, Son of David!"

Matthew 9:27

Mercy is not an emotion, but a practical response to need.

R. T. France

INTRODUCTION

Video Opener from Israel

Scripture Reading: Matthew 9:27–34, followed by a prayer that God will open your heart as you study his Word

Location of Healing: Near Capernaum

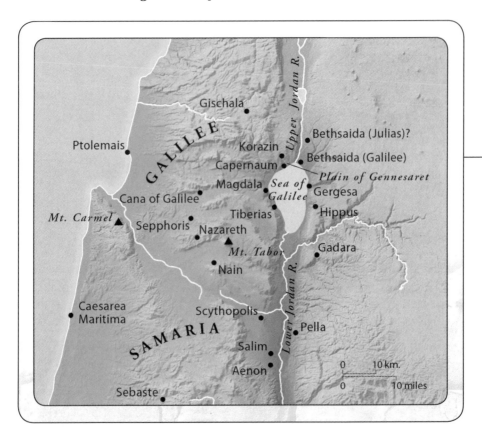

MAKING DEEPER CONNECTIONS TO THE BIBLE

Jesus' miracles show that he is the expected Messiah who brings the kingdom of God, where all illnesses are conquered.

Video Teaching #1 Notes

Location of Video Teaching: Garden of the Gods, Colorado

Garden of the Gods: a location for healing

Miracles and science

> The goodness of God leads him to have a disposition to help humanity. Therefore, sometimes he enters into and acts in history.
>
> Richard Swinburne

True miracle vs. deception

Why do we think the New Testament miracles stories were actual events?

A false assumption

Jesus' miracles were different

Legends in antiquity vs. the dating of the Gospels

The preponderance of evidence suggests that Matthew was published before [AD] 70 ... Mark sometime in the late 50s or the 60s ... and Luke a date in the 60s.

D. A. Carson and Douglas Moo

Even Jesus' opponents admitted he did miracles

DID YOU KNOW?

The giving of sight is a divine activity, and it has messianic significance.

Leon Morris

Men of Israel, listen to this: Jesus of Nazareth was a man accredited by God to you by miracles, wonders and signs, which God did among you through him, as you yourselves know.

Acts 2:22

Why did Jesus do miracles?

Christological: Miracles show who Jesus is

Be strong, do not fear; your God will come, he will come with vengeance; with divine retribution he will come to save you. Then will the eyes of the blind be opened and the ears of the deaf unstopped. Then will the lame leap like a deer, and the mute tongue shout for joy.

Isaiah 35:4–6

Miracles teach about the kingdom of God

> The Spirit of the Lord is on me, because he has anointed me to preach good news to the poor. He has sent me to proclaim freedom for the prisoners and recovery of sight for the blind.
>
> Luke 4:18

Context of Matthew 8–9

Inclusio

> Jesus went throughout Galilee, teaching in their synagogues, preaching the good news of the kingdom, and healing every disease and sickness among the people.
>
> Matthew 4:23 (9:35)

Teaching and healing go hand in hand

Jesus does not just preach the message of good news, he makes it a reality in the lives of individuals through his miracles and exorcisms.

Matt Williams

John the Baptist

Go back and report to John what you *hear* and *see*: The blind receive sight, the lame walk, those who have leprosy are cured, the deaf hear, the dead are raised, and the good news is preached to the poor.

Matthew 11:4–5

Two blind men are healed (Matthew 9:27–31)

Son of David

DID YOU KNOW?

Blindness was one of the grimmest maladies in the ancient world and was considered to be only a little less serious than being dead.

Michael Wilkins

"Do you believe that I am able to do this?" (faith)

Faith is practical confidence in the power of Jesus.

R. T. France

Jesus touches their eyes (healing)

"According to your faith will it be done to you"

> They may have been physically blind, but they "saw" better than many others.
>
> D. A. Carson

"See that no one knows about this"

A mute man is healed (Matthew 9:32–34)

A supernatural power is connected to the physical ailment

> Jesus' healing miracles do not simply remedy human physical maladies, they represent a war against demonic forces.
>
> David Garland

These miracles show that Jesus is the Messiah

DID YOU KNOW?

There was a widespread belief in antiquity in "the king's touch," that is, in the ability of kings to heal their subjects.

W. D. Davies

VIDEO DISCUSSION #1: MAKING DEEPER CONNECTIONS TO THE BIBLE

1. Looking back at the Bible passage and your video teaching notes, what did you learn that you did not know previously? Consider specifically:

   • Reasons for believing that Jesus' miracles were actual events

   • What Jesus' miracles teach us

   • The relationship of teaching to healing

   • The relationship of demons to physical problems

2. What do you think this passage teaches us about the relationship between faith and healing? Do you think that Jesus can heal someone who does not have faith in him? Do you think a person has to reach a certain level of faith before he or she can be healed? Explain.

3. According to Old Testament prophecies, how would people know when they found the Messiah, the Anointed One of God? How do Matthew 4:23 and 9:35 reflect the job description of the Messiah?

4. Why do you think it was obvious to the blind men and the mute man that Jesus was the Son of David, the Messiah, but it was not clear to the Pharisees?

CONNECTING THE BIBLE TO LIFE

Jesus is compassionate, so he wants us to come to him with our needs. But more important than that, he is able to meet our needs because of who he is.

Video Teaching #2 Notes

Jesus, the compassionate One

Jesus preached *and* healed

> He welcomed them [the crowds] and spoke to them about the kingdom of God, and healed those who needed healing.
>
> Luke 9:11

The miracles are meant to confirm the message that in Jesus the power of God's kingdom is breaking into human history.

Mark Strauss

The reaction of the crowds

The reaction of the Pharisees

> But the Pharisees said, "It is by the prince of demons that he drives out demons."
>
> Matthew 9:34

The reactions of people today

What about us?

My own experience

> Do not be anxious about anything, but in everything, by prayer and petition, with thanksgiving, present your requests to God. And the peace of God, which transcends all understanding, will guard your hearts and your minds in Christ Jesus.
>
> Philippians 4:6–7

People today still search for healing in mystical places

Jesus wants us to go to him for healing; we need not hesitate

It has long been fashionable for us to dismiss these gifts as unnecessary or unattainable today. We would be unwise to do so. They are part of God's equipping of his church for evangelism.

Michael Green

When Jesus landed and saw a large crowd, he had compassion on them and healed their sick.

Matthew 14:14

Jesus is the Messiah: he is *able* to meet our needs

Jesus' power can free a person from the evil forces that affect life.

Darrell Bock

VIDEO DISCUSSION #2: CONNECTING THE BIBLE TO LIFE

1. Susan Hecht said that because Jesus is compassionate, we should never hesitate to go to him. Do you normally go to Jesus with your needs, or do you hesitate? Can you think of one example when you hesitated to go to him and one when you did not? What happened in each case?

2. Even though Jesus is the powerful Messiah, able and willing to meet our needs, why do you think that Christians sometimes to try to meet their own needs, as Susan Hecht herself attempted in the example she shared?

3. According to AOL Health, 16 percent of American adults say they have experienced a miraculous physical healing. Do you think that most Christians believe that God performs miracles of healing today? Why or why not? Have you ever experienced a miracle or do you know someone who has? Explain.

4. Why doesn't Jesus always perform miracles when we ask him? Do you find it hard to balance the fact that Jesus has the power to heal us in every way, yet often does not do so? How are his miracles connected to the kingdom of God?

MAKING DEEPER CONNECTIONS IN YOUR OWN LIFE

Personal reflection studies to do on your own

Day One

1. Read Matthew 4:23 and 9:35. Prior to this study, did you think of Jesus' ministry more in terms of preaching/teaching or more in terms of miraculous healing (or equally)? Why do you think you thought as you did?

2. The video lesson taught us to go to Jesus with all of our needs, spiritual as well as physical. How do you tend to deal with needs or difficulties in your life? What does it look like to trust Jesus with those things? What are some ways that Jesus has met your needs in the past? In what ways do you feel that he has *not* met your needs? Spend some prayertime today to take your needs to Jesus.

3. How do you balance the idea of going to Jesus with your needs with the idea of taking responsibility for the things that God has entrusted to you?

Day Two

1. Read Matthew 10:1, 7–8 and 12:22–28.

2. The Jewish leaders were quick to accuse Jesus of healing and casting out demons by the power of evil (see also Matthew 9:32–34). If you had lived in the first century, do you think that you would have been able to figure out if Jesus was healing people by the power of the Spirit of God instead of by the power of evil? What would have helped you to know the difference?

3. What perspective on miracles or the role of miracles has this study suggested to you? Does this correct, clarify, or confirm your previous perspective on miracles? Do you think about or pray about miracles very often? Do you think that Christians today should pray about such things?

Day Three

1. Read Matthew 20:30–34.

2. According to the gospel writers, it was Jesus' compassion that led him to act over and over again. Do you think that God feels compassion toward you? Do your feelings line up with what the Bible says about Jesus' compassion? Spend time in prayer, thanking Jesus for his compassion and asking him to be compassionate toward you in any areas of your life where you need help. List those areas below.

3. Since Jesus is compassionate and able to meet all of our needs, what should be our perspective if he does not meet our needs in ways that we expect? Does that mean he is not compassionate toward us?

Day Four

1. Read Matthew 9:35–38.

2. According to this passage, Jesus' compassion led him to preach and teach as well as heal people of every type of sickness. These verses also depict Jesus putting out the call for more workers. Do you see yourself as one of these "workers" whom God has sent to help others? How could you help people in your family, neighborhood, and community?

3. If Jesus himself experienced mixed responses from people, even to the point that some thought he was in league with demonic forces, what should our expectations be as we seek to minister to others in Jesus' name? What reactions have you experienced as you have ministered to others?

Day Five

1. Read Matthew 9:27–34 one more time.

2. Pray through the entire passage verse by verse, allowing the deeper meaning that you have discovered to lead you as you pray. Ask the Spirit to continue to remind you of what you have learned and to help you apply these truths to your life. Jot down any further applications that come to mind as you pray.

3. Turn back to the discussion questions from the video teaching (Video Discussion #1, #2). If there are questions that your group did not have time to discuss or questions that you might like to think more about, use this time to review and reflect further.

Defeating the Enemy

Jesus Casts Out Demons (Mark 1:21–28)

Dr. Matt Williams

"What do you want with us, Jesus of Nazareth? Have you come to destroy us? I know who you are — the Holy One of God!" "Be quiet!" said Jesus sternly. "Come out of him!"

Mark 1:24–25

The demonic hordes are aware of Jesus' coming and quake in fear at his authority to destroy them.

Mark Strauss

INTRODUCTION

Video Opener from Israel

Synagogue in Capernaum (rebuilt in fourth century AD)

Scripture Reading: Mark 1:21–28, followed by a prayer that God will open your heart as you study his Word

Location of Passage: Synagogue in Capernaum

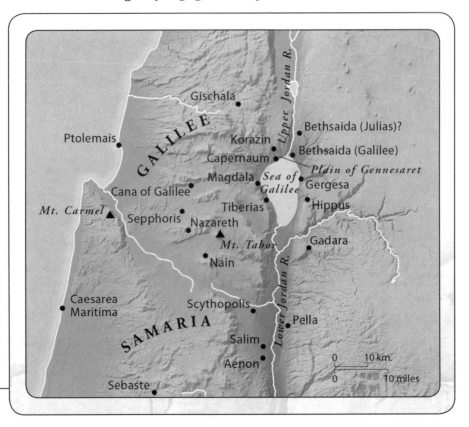

MAKING DEEPER CONNECTIONS TO THE BIBLE

Jesus came to set the prisoners free from demonic bondage.

Video Teaching #1 Notes

Location of Video Teaching: Kay El Bar dude ranch, Wickenburg, Arizona

Jewish people in Jesus' day believed in demons

People today either reduce demons to cartoonlike gremlins or deny their existence completely.

David Garland

Jesus: "The kingdom of heaven is near" (Matthew 4:17)

Satan, the enemy

> The devil is an intelligent, powerful spirit-being that is thoroughly evil and is directly involved in perpetrating evil in the lives of individuals.
>
> Clint Arnold

The reality of demons

But when the Pharisees heard this, they said, "It is only by Beelzebub, the prince of demons, that this fellow drives out demons."

Matthew 12:24

The demons know who Jesus is

I know who you are — the Holy One of God!

Mark 1:24b

Others cast out demons in the first century

Jesus' exorcisms are unique

The deeper meaning of exorcisms

Jesus was taking on his archenemy, Satan

How can anyone enter a strong man's house and carry off his possessions unless he first ties up the strong man? Then he can rob his house.

Matthew 12:29

Exorcisms set people free

> Should not this woman, a daughter of Abraham, whom Satan has kept bound for eighteen long years, be set free on the Sabbath day from what bound her?
>
> Luke 13:16

In the exorcisms of Jesus, Satan is being overpowered and his possessions — people — are being taken from him.

Graham Twelftree

Exorcisms prove the kingdom of God is here

> If I drive out demons by the Spirit of God, then the kingdom of God has come upon you.
>
> Matthew 12:28

Be brave and strong for the battle of God! For this day is the time of the battle of God against all the host of Satan. The God of Israel lifts his hand and his marvelous might against all the spirits of wickedness.

Qumran

Jesus preaches and casts out demons

A sample exorcism (Mark 1:21–28)

The authority of Jesus' teaching

Said R. Aba in the name of R. Jehudah, quoting Samuel: "R. Jehudah subsequently agreed with the sages regarding olives and grapes, and the sages also agreed with him later concerning other fruit." Said R. Jeremiah to R. Aba: "Where do they differ?" and R. Aba answered: "Go and seek, and you will find it!"

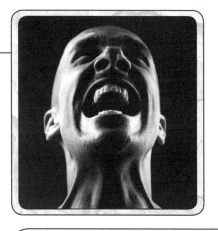

A man cries out

Just then a man in their synagogue who was possessed by an evil spirit cried out.

Mark 1:23

The demons try to overpower Jesus without effect

What do you want with us, Jesus of Nazareth? Have you come to destroy us?

Mark 1:24a

Go away and leave me alone!

R. T. France

Jesus takes command

"Be quiet!"

"said Jesus sternly"

"Jesus said sternly" was a technical phrase that was used to bring evil powers into submission.

Robert Guelich

"Come out of him!" (Mark 1:25)

> The evil spirit shook the man violently and came out of him with a shriek.
>
> Mark 1:26

Jesus disarms Satan's power that has been pirating human souls and sets the victims free one by one.

David Garland

Amazed at Jesus' authority

> The people were all so amazed that they asked each other, "What is this? A new teaching — and with authority! He even gives orders to evil spirits and they obey him."
>
> Mark 1:27

When Jesus grapples with demons, the outcome is never in doubt.

David Garland

VIDEO DISCUSSION #1: MAKING DEEPER CONNECTIONS TO THE BIBLE

1. Looking back at the Bible passage and your video teaching notes, what did you learn that you did not know previously? Consider specifically:

   • Jesus' enemy is not Rome, but Satan

   • The practice of exorcism in the first century

   • The meaning of each part of Mark 1:25: "Be quiet!" said Jesus sternly. "Come out of him!"

2. Matt Williams talked about the "deeper meaning of exorcisms." Were you aware of the three different elements that he mentioned? Discuss the implications of each one.

3. How are Jesus' exorcisms different than the exorcisms of other first-century exorcists?

4. Do you think that only Jesus has authority to cast out demons, or do you think he has given this same authority to Christians today? What biblical and experiential evidence can you give to support your answer?

CONNECTING THE BIBLE TO LIFE

Christians, in union with Christ, share in his triumph over Satan.

Video Teaching #2 Notes

Dodgeball victory

Jesus' victory at the cross

Having disarmed the powers and authorities, he made a public spectacle of them, triumphing over them by the cross.

Colossians 2:15

Satan is ticked

> Woe to the earth and the sea, because the devil has gone down to you! He is filled with fury, because he knows that his time is short.
>
> Revelation 12:12

Many act like demons don't exist

> Your enemy the devil prowls around like a roaring lion looking for someone to devour.
>
> 1 Peter 5:8

Jesus' disciples cast out demons

> He appointed twelve — designating them apostles — that they might be with him and that he might send them out to preach and to have authority to drive out demons.
>
> Mark 3:14–15
>
> ─────── ◉ ───────
>
> I saw Satan fall like lightning from heaven.
>
> Luke 10:18

The early church cast out demons

Satan has two strategies

> Your enemy the devil prowls around like a roaring *lion* looking for someone to devour.
>
> 1 Peter 5:8
>
> ――――――――――――――――――――――
>
> Satan himself masquerades as an *angel of light*.
>
> 2 Corinthians 11:14

Modern evangelical leaders

We live in a perpetual battlefield. The wars among the nations on earth are mere popgun affairs compared to the fierceness of battle in the spiritual unseen world.

Billy Graham

My experience

Balance!

> There are two equal and opposite errors into which our race can fall about the devils. One is to disbelieve in their existence. The other is to believe, and feel an excessive and unhealthy interest in them. They themselves are equally pleased by both errors.
>
> C. S. Lewis

Variety of experiences in casting out demons

Physical, psychological, or demonic

> The attempt to explain phenomena once ascribed to evil spirits exclusively in medical or psychological terms seems to have failed. There remains a residue of phenomena that is unexplained.
>
> Graham Twelftree

Pray

> After Jesus had gone indoors, his disciples asked him privately, "Why couldn't we drive it out?" He replied, "This kind can come out only by prayer."
>
> Mark 9:28–29

Face spiritual warfare with God's authority

> I have given you authority . . . to overcome all the power of the enemy; nothing will harm you.
>
> Luke 10:19
>
> ———————————— ⊚ ————————————
>
> The one who is in you is greater than the one who is in the world.
>
> 1 John 4:4

Satan's evil forces will continue to be confronted, as Jesus' emissaries go out with his authority to bring release to the harassed and helpless.

Michael Wilkins

The full armor of God

Put on the full armor of God so that you can take your stand against the devil's schemes.

Ephesians 6:11

Compassionately setting people free

I will build my church, and the gates of Hades will not overcome it.

Matthew 16:18

Exorcism is a battle in which people illegitimately held by Satan are taken, so that Satan is seen to be overthrown.

Graham Twelftree

VIDEO DISCUSSION #2: CONNECTING THE BIBLE TO LIFE

1. Do you think that demons exist today? What evidence would you give—both biblical and experiential—to support your answer? How do they tend to operate in your geographical area—more like a lion or an angel of light?

2. Have you ever experienced spiritual warfare or known someone who has? What was it like? Do you think that spiritual warfare is always really wild, or could it also be evidenced by a bad attitude or conflicts with other Christians at church?

3. If demons are real, and Satan still binds people (as in Luke 13:16), do you think that part of Christian ministry is setting people free from demonic oppression? Why or why not?

4. What do you think would happen to a Christian who gets involved in spiritual warfare, specifically exorcisms, but does not protect him- or herself with God's armor (see Ephesians 6)?

MAKING DEEPER CONNECTIONS IN YOUR OWN LIFE

Personal reflection studies to do on your own

Day One

1. Read Luke 10:1–20. Notice the relationship between the mission of preaching the kingdom of God and showing that the kingdom has come through the miraculous.

2. Reflect on the authority and power of Jesus over all things, including spiritual forces. Thank him for being your protector, then list below the different ways that he protects you, maybe even in specific situations you have encountered in the past.

3. Do you think that Jesus still gives authority to Christians today to cast out demons, or was that just for the early church? What evidence would you give to support your answer? If Jesus gives us Christians authority to "overcome the enemy" (Luke 10:19), do you think that we can ever lose a battle? Why or why not?

Day Two

1. Read Ephesians 6:10–18.

2. As with any battle, spiritual warfare has two components: defensive and offensive. As you read Ephesians 6:10–18, notice that each piece of armor can be designated either for a defensive or offensive purpose. Do you often reflect on the power of prayer, the shield of faith, and the other weapons that God has given you to help protect yourself from the enemy's "flaming arrows"? What would happen to you if you did not protect yourself with God's armor?

3. The Gospels also teach that God has equipped us for advancing into enemy territory to reclaim people for the kingdom of God. Was Satan's defeat totally accomplished at the cross, or must he be defeated in individual battles as we live here on the earth? How often do you think about going to battle against the enemy? What "weapons" could you use?

Day Three

1. Read 2 Kings 6:14–17.

2. Matt Williams mentioned that the topic of casting out demons is quite complex. Today is a day to reflect on your need for further study. What are the main questions related to this topic that you still struggle with? Jot them down here.

3. Do online searches of the spiritual warfare titles provided in the bibliography at the end of this participant's guide. If you were going to study this topic further, what books would you begin with? Consider picking up one or two of these sometime soon.

Day Four

1. Read Luke 13:10–17 and Mark 1:21–28.

2. According to Mark 1:23–24, a demon cried out in the synagogue. Do you think that demons influence and attack people in our "synagogues," the church? What would this look like? Do you

ever ask for protection before a Bible study, church services, or prayer meeting? Why or why not?

3. Use part of your prayer time to ask God's protection on those gatherings of his people that you regularly attend.

Day Five

1. Read Mark 1:21–28 one more time.

2. Pray through the entire passage verse by verse, allowing the deeper meaning that you have discovered to lead you as you pray. Ask the Spirit to continue to remind you of what you have learned and to help you apply these truths to your life. Jot down any further applications that come to mind as you pray.

3. Turn back to the discussion questions from the video teaching (Video Discussion #1, #2). If there are questions that your group did not have time to discuss or questions that you might like to think more about, use this time to review and reflect further.

Source Acknowledgments

(These are noted in order of appearance for each session. Full source information can be found in "Books for Further Reading" beginning on page 139.)

Session 1

Page 11: Hagner, *Matthew*, 22.
Page 13: Walker, *Steps of Jesus*, 28.
Page 16: Bock, *Jesus According to Scriptures*, 59.
Page 16: France, *Matthew*, 51.
Page 17: Bailey, *Jesus through Middle Eastern Eyes*, 37.
Page 18: Blomberg, *Matthew*, 62.
Page 22: Hagner, *Matthew*, 31.
Page 23: Bock, *Luke*, NIVAC, 84.

Session 2

Page 31: Strauss, *Luke*, 41.
Page 33: Walker, *Steps of Jesus*, 43.
Page 36: Ibid., 45.
Page 37: Turner, *Matthew*, 114.
Page 38: Walker, *Steps of Jesus*, 45.
Page 38: France, *Matthew*, 121.
Page 39: Evans, *Bible Knowledge*, 78.
Page 42: Garland, *Mark*, NIVAC, 57.
Page 44: Bock, *Luke*, NIVAC, 115.
Page 44: Wilkins, *Matthew*, NIVAC, 152.
Page 45: Wilkins, *Matthew*, ZIBBC, 27.

Session 3

Page 53: Walker, *Steps of Jesus*, 64.

Page 55: Morris, *Luke*, 109.
Page 56: Strauss, *Luke*, 43.
Page 56: Blomberg, *Matthew*, 83.
Page 57: Evans, *Bible Knowledge*, 82.
Page 58: Bock, *Luke*, 378.
Page 60: Bock, *Luke*, NIVAC, 128.
Page 60: Wilkins, *Matthew*, NIVAC, 160.
Page 64: Bock, *Luke*, NIVAC, 131.
Page 65: Ibid., 376.
Page 65: Blomberg, *Matthew*, 85.
Page 66: Wilkins, *Matthew*, NIVAC, 160.
Page 67: Ibid., 161.

Session 4

Page 75: Blomberg, *Jesus Gospels*, 234.
Page 78: Bock, *Luke*, NIVAC, 154.
Page 78: Garland, *Mark*, NIVAC, 84.
Page 80: Blomberg, *Jesus Gospels*, 234.
Page 80: Stein, *Jesus the Messiah*, 114.
Page 82: Garland, *Mark*, NIVAC, 69.
Page 84: Strauss, *Luke*, 53.
Page 85: Wilkins, *Matthew*, NIVAC, 187.

Session 5

Page 91: France, *Matthew*, Tyndale, 172.
Page 93: Swinburne, *In Defense of Miracles*, 193.
Page 94: Carson and Moo, *An Introduction to the New Testament* (Zondervan, 2005), 156, 182, 208.
Page 95: Morris, *Matthew*, 233.
Page 98: Wilkins, *Matthew*, NIVAC, 372.
Page 98: France, *Matthew*, Tyndale, 172.
Page 99: Carson, *Matthew*, 233.
Page 100: Garland, Mark, 71.
Page 100: Davies, *Matthew*, 137.
Page 103: Strauss, *Luke*, 48.
Page 104: http://www.cleveland.com/nation/index.ssf/2008/08/majority_of_americans_believe.html.
Page 105: Green, *Evangelism and the Early Church* (Eerdmans, 2004), 26–27.
Page 105: Bock, *Luke*, 442.

Session 6

Page 113: Strauss, *Luke*, 49.

Page 115: Garland, *Mark*, 79.

Page 116: Arnold, *Three Crucial Questions about Spiritual War* (Baker, 1997), 35.

Page 118: Twelftree, *Name of Jesus*, 95.

Page 118: Qumran quote: Twelftree, *Jesus Exorcist*, 50.

Page 119: http://www.sacred-texts.com/jud/t01/t0134.htm.

Page 120: France, *Mark*, 103.

Page 120: Guelich, *Mark*, 57.

Page 121: Garland, *Mark*, 71.

Page 121: Ibid., 54.

Page 126: Graham, *Angels: God's Secret Agents* (Doubleday, 1975), 66.

Page 127: Lewis, *The Screwtape Letters* (Macmillan, 1961), 3.

Page 127: Twelftree, *Christ Triumphant*, 155.

Page 128: Wilkins, *Matthew*, NIVAC, 377.

Page 129: Twelftree, *Name of Jesus*, 114.

Map and Photo Credits

Maps: Courtesy of International Mapping

Joe Beattie: page 115

Jace Doron: page 92

Doug Green: page 36

Jane Haradine: pages 38 (bottom), 67, 126

T. J. Rathbun: pages 13, 32, 33, 54, 57, 77, 84 (top), 114

Andy Sheneman: pages 11, 31, 53, 75, 91, 113

istockphoto.com: pages 14, 16, 17, 18, 21, 22, 23, 34, 37, 38 (top), 39, 40, 42, 43, 56, 58, 59, 61, 64, 66, 79, 80, 82, 84 (bottom), 94, 95, 96, 98, 100, 102, 104, 116, 117, 119, 121, 123, 128, 129

Books for Further Reading

Miracles

Brown, Colin. *Miracles and the Critical Mind.* Grand Rapids, Mich.: Eerdmans, 1984.

Geivett, R. Douglas and Gary R. Habermas. *In Defense of Miracles: A Comprehensive Case for God's Action in History.* Downers Grove, Ill.: InterVarsity Press, 1997.

Lewis, C. S. *Miracles.* San Francisco: HarperSanFrancisco, 2001.

Moreland, J. P. *The Kingdom Triangle.* Grand Rapids, Mich.: Zondervan, 2007.

Wenham, David and Craig Blomberg, eds. *The Miracles of Jesus.* Sheffield, England: JSOT Press, 1986.

Wilkins, Michael J. and J. P. Moreland, eds. *Jesus Under Fire.* Grand Rapids, Mich.: Zondervan, 1995.

Exorcisms

Anderson, Neil T. and Timothy M. Warner. *The Beginner's Guide to Spiritual Warfare.* Ventura, Calif.: Regal, 2000.

Arnold, Clinton. *Three Crucial Questions about Spiritual Warfare.* Grand Rapids, Mich.: Baker, 1997.

Deere, Jack. *Surprised by the Power of the Spirit.* Grand Rapids, Mich.: Zondervan, 1993.

Kraft, Charles H. *Defeating Dark Angels: Breaking Demonic Oppression in the Believer's Life.* Ann Arbor, Mich.: Vine, 1992.

Kraft, Charles H. *I Give You Authority: Practicing the Authority Jesus Gave Us.* Grand Rapids, Mich.: Chosen, 1997.

Twelftree, Graham H. *In the Name of Jesus: Exorcism among Early Christians.* Grand Rapids, Mich.: Baker, 2007.

_____. *Jesus the Exorcist: A Contribution to the Study of the Historical Jesus*. Peabody, Mass.: Hendrickson, 1993.

Life of Jesus

Bailey, Kenneth E. *Jesus through Middle Eastern Eyes: Cultural Studies in the Gospels*. Downers Grove, Ill.: InterVarsity, 2008.

Blomberg, Craig L. *Jesus and the Gospels: An Introduction and Survey*. Nashville: Broadman and Holman, 1997.

Bock, Darrell L. *Jesus According to Scripture: Restoring the Portrait from the Gospels*. Grand Rapids, Mich.: Baker, 2002.

Stein, Robert H. *Jesus the Messiah: A Survey of the Life of Christ*. Downers Grove, Ill.: InterVarsity, 1996.

Strauss, Mark L. *Four Portraits, One Jesus: An Introduction to Jesus and the Gospels*. Grand Rapids, Mich.: Zondervan, 2007.

Walker, Peter. *In the Steps of Jesus: An Illustrated Guide to the Places of the Holy Land*. Grand Rapids, Mich.: Zondervan, 2006.

Four Gospels

Beale, G. K. and D. A. Carson. *Commentary on the New Testament Use of the Old Testament*. Grand Rapids, Mich.: Baker, 2007.

Evans, Craig A., gen. ed. *The Bible Knowledge Background Commentary: Matthew–Luke*. Colorado Springs: Victor Books, 2003.

Keener, Craig S. *The IVP Bible Background Commentary: New Testament*. Downers Grove, Ill.: InterVarsity Press, 1993.

Kroeger, Catherine Clark and Mary J. Evans, eds. *The IVP Women's Bible Commentary*. Downers Grove, Ill.: InterVarsity Press, 2002.

Matthew

Barton, Bruce B. *Matthew*. Life Application Bible Commentary. Wheaton, Ill.: Tyndale, 1996.

Blomberg, Craig L. *Matthew*. New American Commentary, vol. 22. Nashville, Tenn.: Broadman Press, 1992.

Carson, D. A. *Matthew, Mark, Luke*. The Expositor's Bible Commentary, vol. 8. Grand Rapids, Mich.: Zondervan, 1984.

Davies, W. D., Dale C. Allison Jr. *A Critical and Exegetical Commentary on the Gospel According to Saint Matthew*. The International Critical Commentary. 3 vols. Edinburgh: T. & T. Clark, 1988, 1991, 1997.

France, R. T. *The Gospel According to Matthew: An Introduction and Commentary*. Tyndale New Testament Commentaries, vol. 1. Grand Rapids, Mich.: Eerdmans, 1985.

France, R. T. *The Gospel of Matthew*. The New International Commentary on the New Testament. Grand Rapids, Mich.: Eerdmans, 2007.

Green, Michael. *The Message of Matthew: The Kingdom of Heaven*. The Bible Speaks Today Series. Downers Grove, Ill.: InterVarsity Press, 2000.

Guelich, Robert A. *Sermon on the Mount: A Foundation for Understanding*. Waco, Tex.: Word, 1982.

Gundry, Robert. *Matthew: A Commentary on His Handbook for a Mixed Church Under Persecution*. Grand Rapids, Mich.: W.B. Eerdmans, 2nd ed., 1994.

Hagner, Donald. *Matthew*. Word Biblical Commentary, vol. 33 a&b. Waco, Tex.: Word, 1993, 1995.

Keener, Craig S. *A Commentary on the Gospel of Matthew*. Grand Rapids, Mich.: Eerdmans, 1999.

Morris, Leon. *The Gospel According to Matthew*. The Pillar New Testament Commentary. Grand Rapids, Mich.: Eerdmans, 1992.

Mounce, Robert H. *Matthew*. New International Biblical Commentary, vol. 1. Peabody, Mass.: Hendrickson, 1991.

Nolland, John. *The Gospel of Matthew: A Commentary on the Greek Text*. The New International Greek Testament Commentary. Grand Rapids, Mich.: Eerdmans, 2005.

Simonetti, Manlio, ed. *Matthew*. Ancient Christian Commentary on Scripture. 2 vols. Downers Grove, Ill.: InterVarsity Press, 2002.

Turner, David L. *Matthew*. Baker Exegetical Commentary on the New Testament. Grand Rapids, Mich.: Baker, 2008.

Turner, David L. and Darrell L. Bock. *The Gospel of Matthew/The Gospel of Mark*. Cornerstone Biblical Commentary. Wheaton, Ill.: Tyndale, 2006.

Wilkins, Michael J. *Matthew: From Biblical Text to Contemporary Life*. The NIV Application Commentary. Grand Rapids, Mich.: Zondervan, 2004.

_____. *Zondervan Illustrated Bible Backgrounds Commentary*. Grand Rapids, Mich.: Zondervan, 2002.

Mark

Cole, R. Alan. *The Gospel According to Mark*. Tyndale New Testament Commentaries, vol. 2. Grand Rapids, Mich.: Eerdmans, 2002.

Cranfield, C. E. B. *The Gospel According to Saint Mark: An Introduction and Commentary*. Cambridge Greek Testament Commentary. Cambridge University Press, 1972.

Edwards, James R. *The Gospel According to Mark*. The Pillar New Testament Commentary. Grand Rapids, Mich.: Eerdmans, 2002.

Evans, Craig. *Mark*. Word Biblical Commentary, vol. 34b. Nashville: Thomas Nelson, 2001.

Fackler, Mark. *Mark*. Life Application Bible Commentary. Wheaton, Ill.: Tyndale, 1994.

France, R. T. *The Gospel of Mark: A Commentary on the Greek Text*. The New International Greek New Testament Commentary. Grand Rapids, Mich.: Eerdmans, 2002.

Garland, David E. *Mark*. The NIV Application Commentary. Grand Rapids, Mich.: Zondervan, 1996.

————. *Zondervan Illustrated Bible Backgrounds Commentary*. Grand Rapids, Mich.: Zondervan, 2002.

Guelich, Robert A. *Mark*. Word Biblical Commentary, vol. 34a. Dallas: Word, 1989.

Gundry, Robert H. *A Commentary on His Apology for the Cross*. Grand Rapids, Mich.: Eerdmans, 1993.

Lane, William L. *The Gospel According to Mark: The English Text with Introduction, Exposition, and Notes*. The New International Commentary on the New Testament. Grand Rapids, Mich.: Eerdmans, 1974.

McKenna, David L. *Mark*. The Communicator's Commentary Series, vol. 2. Dallas: Word, 1982.

Oden, Thomas C. and Christopher A. Hall, eds. *Mark*. Ancient Christian Commentary on Scripture, vol. 2. Downers Grove, Ill.: InterVarsity Press, 1998.

Stein, Robert H. *Mark*. Baker Exegetical Commentary on the New Testament. Grand Rapids, Mich.: Baker, 2008.

Taylor, Vincent. *The Gospel According to St. Mark: The Greek Text with Introduction, Notes, and Indexes*. Thornapple Commentaries. Grand Rapids, Mich.: Baker, 2nd ed., 1981.

Wessel, Walter W. *Matthew, Mark, Luke*. The Expositor's Bible Commentary, vol. 8. Grand Rapids, Mich.: Zondervan, 1984.

Witherington, Ben III. *The Gospel of Mark: A Socio-Rhetorical Commentary*. Grand Rapids, Mich.: Eerdmans, 2001.

Luke

Barton, Bruce B., Dave Veerman, and Linda K. Taylor. *Luke*. Life Application Bible Commentary. Wheaton, Ill.: Tyndale, 1997.

Bock, Darrell L. *Luke*. The NIV Application Commentary Series. Grand Rapids, Mich.: Zondervan, 1996.

Bock, Darrell L. *Luke 1:1:1 – 9:50; 9:51 – 24:53*. Baker Exegetical Commentary on the New Testament, 2 vols. Grand Rapids, Mich.: Baker, 1996.

Evans, Craig A. *Luke*. New International Biblical Commentary, vol. 3. Peabody, Mass.: Hendrickson, 1990.

Fitzmyer, J. A. *The Gospel According to Luke: Introduction, Translation, and Notes.* Anchor Bible, vol. 28–28a. Garden City, N.Y.: Doubleday, 1981–1985.

Green, Joel B. *The Gospel of Luke.* New International Commentary on the New Testament. Grand Rapids, Mich.: Eerdmans, 1997.

Just, Arther A. Jr., ed. *Luke.* Ancient Christian Commentary on Scripture, vol. 3. Downers Grove, Ill.: InterVarsity Press, 2003.

Larson, Bruce. *Luke.* The Preacher's Commentary, vol. 26. Nashville: Thomas Nelson, 1983.

Liefeld, Walter L. *Matthew, Mark, Luke.* The Expositor's Bible Commentary, vol. 8. Grand Rapids, Mich.: Zondervan, 1984.

Marshall, I. Howard. *Luke: Historian and Theologian.* Grand Rapids, Mich.: Zondervan, 1980.

Morris, Leon. *Luke, An Introduction and Commentary.* Tyndale New Testament Commentaries, vol. 3. Grand Rapids, Mich.: Eerdmans, 1988.

Nolland, John. *Luke.* Word Biblical Commentary, vol. 35a–c. Dallas: Word, 1989–1993.

Stein, Robert H. *Luke.* The New American Commentary, vol. 24. Nashville: Broadman, 1992.

Strauss, Mark L. *Luke.* Zondervan Illustrated Bible Backgrounds Commentary. Grand Rapids, Mich.: Zondervan, 2002.

John

Barrett, C. K. *The Gospel According to St. John: An Introduction with Commentary and Notes on the Greek Text.* Philadelphia: Westminster Press, 1978.

Barton, Bruce B. *John.* Life Application Bible Commentary. Wheaton, Ill.: Tyndale, 1993.

Beasley-Murray, George R. *John.* Word Biblical Commentaries, vol. 36. Nashville: Thomas Nelson, 1999.

Brown, Raymond Edward. *The Gospel According to John.* Anchor Bible, vol. 29–29a. Garden City, N.Y.: Doubleday, 1966–1970.

Burge, Gary M. *John.* The NIV Application Commentary. Grand Rapids, Mich.: Zondervan, 2000.

Card, Michael. *The Parable of Joy: Reflections on the Wisdom of the Book of John.* Nashville: Thomas Nelson, 1995.

Carson, Donald A. *The Gospel According to John.* The Pillar New Testament Commentary. Grand Rapids, Mich.: Eerdmans, 1991.

Keener, Craig S. *The Gospel of John: A Commentary.* 2 vols. Peabody, Mass.: Hendrickson, 2003.

Köstenberger, Andreas J. *John*. Baker Exegetical Commentary on the New Testament. Grand Rapids, Mich.: Baker, 2004.

_____. *Zondervan Illustrated Bible Backgrounds Commentary*. Grand Rapids, Mich.: Zondervan, 2002.

Morris, Leon. *The Gospel According to John*. New International Commentary on the New Testament. Grand Rapids, Mich.: Eerdmans, 1995.

Osborne, Grant R. *The Gospel of John*. Cornerstone Biblical Commentary, vol. 13. Carol Stream, Ill.: Tyndale, 2007.

Tasker, R. V. G. *The Gospel According to St. John: An Introduction and Commentary*. Tyndale New Testament Commentaries. Grand Rapids, Mich.: Eerdmans, 1960.

Tenney, Merrill C. *John, Acts*. The Expositor's Bible Commentary, vol. 9. Grand Rapids, Mich.: Zondervan, 1984.

Whitacre, Rodney A. *John*. The IVP New Testament Commentary Series, vol. 4. Downers Grove, Ill.: InterVarsity Press, 1999.